Price Action

Madelyn Price

Copyright Page

Copyright Holder: © 2024, Andrea Jimenez
Year: 2024
Author: © 2024, Madelyn Price

Legal and Copyright Information

First edition
All Rights Reserved

Index

Introduction to Price Action

Price action is, at its core, the analysis of price movement in the market, without the need to rely on additional indicators or technical tools. In its purest form, it is about observing how price behaves over time, how it rises and falls, how it pauses and how it accelerates. This information, when understood correctly, can offer clear insight into what is happening in the market and what might happen next. Price action is like learning a new language, but instead of words and sentences, you are interpreting charts and candles.

To understand price action, the first thing to recognize is that financial markets are driven by two fundamental emotions: fear and greed. When the price goes up, buyers are showing their optimism about the future of an asset; when the price goes down, sellers are showing their fear that things could get worse. Price action reflects these human feelings in the form of charts. Traders who are able to understand and read those charts are, in a way, tapping into the collective mind of the market. They are seeing the decisions of thousands or even millions of market participants expressed on a chart.

It's not just about looking at green and red candles on a chart. Each of those candles tells a story about the interaction between buyers and sellers. When you learn to interpret those stories, you can make informed decisions without the need to confuse yourself with indicators that often end up overwhelming your analysis. Price action takes you back to basics: price is the most important indicator. This approach is as old as the market itself, and has been used by traders for decades, if not centuries, to gain an edge in their trading.

Imagine that you are looking at the market as a battlefield. Buyers and sellers are constantly fighting for control, and price action shows you who is winning that battle at any given moment. Big rallies can show that buyers are taking control, while sharp declines indicate that sellers are in power. However, there are times when the market takes a breather. The price may move sideways, showing no clear winner.

This is the moment when patient traders know that something is about to happen.

The fascinating thing about price action is that you don't need to have a ton of tools or indicators to be successful. In fact, many experienced traders choose to ditch all the indicators and simply look at price charts in their purest form. By cutting out the noise, you can better focus on what really matters: price action. This doesn't mean price action is easy, but it does mean it's a more direct and honest approach. It's analysis at its most basic, with no distractions.

There is something really liberating about learning to read price this way. Many new traders feel overwhelmed by the number of indicators available: moving averages, RSI, MACD, and many others. These indicators can be helpful in some cases, but the reality is that they are all price-based. Instead of relying on a lagging version of information, as indicators do, price action shows you what is happening in the moment. You don't need to wait for an indicator to tell you that price has gone up when you can see it right on the chart.

It is important to note that price action is not a magic formula that will tell you with certainty where the market will move. What it does is give you a clear idea of the context of the market, of who is winning and losing at the moment. By looking at patterns on the chart, such as single candles or series of them, you can start to see the signs of possible changes in direction or continuations in the current trend. All of this is based on pure observation of how the price has acted in the past and how it is likely to act in the future.

Price action is applicable in any market: from stocks to currencies, cryptocurrencies or futures. No matter what you're trading, price is still price. Learning to read it effectively can give you an edge over those traders who rely solely on complex indicators. Big moves in the market may seem random at first, but once you start interpreting price action, they become much more understandable.

Mastering price action takes time and practice. It requires you to look closely at the charts and, most importantly, to trust what you see. Many times, new traders are tempted to add more indicators to confirm their decisions. However, traders who focus on price action learn to trust their eyes and their ability to interpret the chart. It's not about perfection, but about constantly improving your ability to read the market in its purest form.

In short, price action is a powerful and straightforward tool that allows you to understand the market through the movement of price itself. You don't need to complicate your analysis with overstuffed indicators or complex strategies. By focusing on price action, you are learning to read the true story that the market is telling in real time. Although it may seem like a simple approach, it is one that has stood the test of time and continues to be used by traders around the world with great success.

Understanding Japanese Candlestick Charts

Japanese candlestick charts are one of the most popular and effective tools for understanding price action in the market. At first glance, they may seem confusing or full of meaningless details, but once you understand how they work, they become a clear and visual way to read what is happening with the price. Each candlestick on a chart represents a specific time period, and within that time, it shows the complete history of what happened with the price: from the highest level reached to the lowest level, as well as the opening and closing price.

To break down a candlestick into its parts, the first thing you need to look at is the body. The body is the central part of the candlestick, and its color (usually green or red) tells you whether the price rose or fell during that period. If the candlestick is green, it means that the price closed higher than it opened, indicating that buyers were in control. If the candlestick is red, it means that the price closed lower than it opened, suggesting that sellers had the upper hand. This simple detail already gives you a quick overview of who dominated the market during that time.

In addition to the body, candles have what are known as "wicks" or "shadows," which are those thin lines that come out from the top or bottom of the candle's body. The upper wick shows the highest price that was reached during that period, while the lower wick represents the lowest price. Wicks can give you important clues about what's going on behind the scenes in the market. For example, if a candle has a long upper wick, it means that the price rose a lot during that period, but it couldn't hold there and ended up falling before the candle closed. This can be a sign that sellers started to take control after a brief bullish push.

One of the reasons why Japanese candlestick charts are so useful is because they can show market emotions in a visual way. When a candlestick has a large, solid body, either green or red, it indicates that there was a strong decision by market participants. On a large green candlestick, buyers clearly won, while on a large red candlestick, sellers dominated without much resistance. On the other hand, if a candlestick has a small body, that can indicate indecision. Neither buyers nor sellers managed to have significant control during that period.

There are certain patterns in Japanese candlesticks that traders have learned to recognize and that can give clues as to what might happen next in the market. One of the most basic patterns is the "doji," a candlestick that has an extremely small body, indicating that the opening price and closing price were almost at the same level. A doji candlestick suggests indecision in the market. Buyers and sellers battled it out, but in the end neither clearly won. When you see a doji after a strong trend, it can be a sign that momentum is weakening and there could be a change in direction soon.

Another common pattern is the "hammer" and "hanging man" candles, which are candles with small bodies and long wicks, either at the top or bottom. The hammer has a long wick down and a small body at the top, indicating that the price dropped a lot during the period, but buyers managed to push it back up before the candle closed. This can be a sign that buyers are starting to gain strength after a period of selling. The hanging man, on the other hand, has a long wick up and a small body at the bottom, suggesting that although buyers tried to push the price up, sellers managed to push it back down before the close. This can be a sign that the market is losing bullish momentum.

One of the great benefits of Japanese candlestick charts is that they allow you to see patterns across multiple candles, giving you a more complete picture of what is going on. For example, the "bullish engulfing" pattern occurs when a large green candle completely engulfs a smaller red candle before it. This can be a sign that buyers have taken control after a period of selling. Similarly, the "bearish engulfing" pattern is the opposite: a large red candle engulfing a smaller green candle, suggesting that sellers have gained ground and could be ready to push the price down.

Using Japanese candlestick charts isn't limited to just individual patterns. It's also critical to look at the relationship between candles within the overall context of the market. Sometimes a candle that might seem significant on its own isn't all that important when you put it into the bigger picture. For example, if you're looking at a strongly uptrend market and a red candle appears, that may not be a red flag on its own, as it may simply be a small correction within a broader trend. But if you see multiple red candles in a row, or if certain key patterns such as a bearish engulfing appear, that can indicate that momentum is changing.

Another thing to keep in mind when using Japanese candlestick charts is that they work on any time frame. Whether you are trading on 1-minute, 5-minute, daily, or even weekly charts, Japanese candlesticks will show you the same essential information. This makes this tool extremely versatile as you can adapt it to any trading style you prefer. Both intraday traders, swing traders, or even long-term investors can benefit from understanding how to read and analyze candlesticks.

In short, candlestick charts are a powerful tool for interpreting price action in a clear and straightforward manner. Through candlestick shapes, colors, bodies, and wicks, you can learn to read what the market is doing and, more importantly, what it might do next. Whether looking at a single candle or looking for more complex patterns, candlesticks offer unique insight into price action, giving you the information you need to make informed trading decisions. While it may seem overwhelming at first, with practice, you'll learn to read these charts as if you were reading a book full of stories about market behavior.

Identification of Key Areas

Identifying key zones is one of the fundamental pillars of price action analysis. These key zones are places on the chart where the price tends to react significantly. In most cases, these areas correspond to support and resistance levels, which act as barriers that the price encounters along its path. For traders, understanding where these levels are located is crucial, as it is in these areas that the most important decisions usually occur, both to enter and exit a trade.

Support is an area on the chart where the price tends to stop when it goes down. Basically, it is a level where buyers start to step in strongly, preventing the price from falling further. Think of support as the floor of a room: when a ball falls, it inevitably stops on the floor and, in many cases, bounces back up. In a market, this "ball" is the price, and support is that place where buyers decide that the price has fallen far enough and start buying, causing the price to rise again. Identifying these levels can help you find good buying points, as it is in these places that demand often outstrips supply.

On the other hand, resistance is the opposite of support. Resistance is a level where price tends to stop when it goes up. Imagine it as the ceiling of a room: when the ball is thrown up, it will eventually hit the ceiling and bounce back down. In the case of the market, this "ceiling" is resistance, where sellers start to act, convinced that the price has already gone up enough and now it is time to sell. When price reaches this zone, it is common to see the market stop, and often begin a decline, as supply outstrips demand.

The interesting thing about key support and resistance zones is that they are not exact points on the chart, but rather areas. This means that rather than waiting for price to hit an exact level and then pull back, you should think of them as zones where price has a higher probability of reacting. This flexibility is important because the market is rarely that precise. Sometimes price can get very close to a support or resistance level and then reverse before touching it, or sometimes it can breach that level briefly before turning back. So it's critical to understand that these are areas of importance and not perfect lines.

To properly identify key zones, the first step is to look at previous highs and lows on the chart. If the price has touched a certain zone several times in the past and has pulled back each time, that zone has a high probability of being a strong support or resistance. This is because these levels represent places where the market has shown significant interest in slowing down or changing direction. For example, if an asset has touched the same price area three or four times and each time it does so, the price bounces back up, then you can be sure that that is an important support level.

A key concept is that support and resistance can reverse roles. This happens when price breaks a support or resistance level and then retests it from the other side. For example, if price breaks below a support, that support may become resistance in the future. Likewise, if price breaks above a resistance, that resistance could act as support in the future. This phenomenon is known as "polarity reversal," and it is a valuable tool for traders, as it offers additional opportunities to enter or exit the market in places where there were previously significant barriers.

Another thing to keep in mind is that not all support and resistance levels are of equal strength. Some are more significant than others, and the key to good analysis is learning to distinguish between them. Generally, levels that have been touched many times are stronger than those that have only been touched once or twice. Also, levels that have withstood very large or strong price moves tend to be stronger. The more times the price has bounced off a key zone, the greater the likelihood that that zone will be important in the future.

To identify key zones, you don't need to use complicated indicators. You can do this by simply looking at the chart in its most basic form. Experienced traders can often spot support and resistance simply by observing price action. However, if you prefer a more visual approach, there are tools on trading platforms that allow you to draw horizontal lines at levels where the price has shown significant reactions. These lines can act as reminders of levels to watch out for as you analyze the market.

One fascinating thing about key zones is that they apply across all time frames. No matter if you are trading on 1-minute, 15-minute, daily, or weekly charts, support and resistance levels are still relevant. On shorter time frames, you can identify key zones for quick trades, while on longer time frames, those same key zones can help you establish benchmarks for longer-term trends. This makes key zone analysis extremely versatile and useful for any type of trader.

Once you have identified the key zones, the next step is to use them to make trading decisions. For example, if the price is approaching a support zone, you can consider making a buy with the expectation that the price will bounce off that zone. On the other hand, if the price is approaching a resistance zone, you can consider selling or at least be prepared for a possible reversal. You can also use these zones to place your stop-loss and take-profit more effectively. For example, if you are buying in a support zone, you could place your stop-loss just below that zone in case the price breaks it.

In short, identifying key zones is an essential skill for any trader who wants to trade based on price action. Support and resistance provide you with important reference points where price has a higher probability of stopping or changing direction. By learning to identify these zones and using them in your trading strategies, you will be better equipped to make informed decisions and manage risk effectively. Although it may seem simple, mastering key zone identification can make a huge difference in your ability to read the market and find profitable opportunities.

Reading the Market Address

Reading market direction is an essential skill that every trader needs to develop. Understanding where the market is headed is critical to making sound decisions and, ultimately, being profitable in your trading. People often feel overwhelmed by the amount of information they receive when looking at a chart: candlesticks, sharp moves, retracements. But the truth is, reading market direction is based on simple concepts. The market can move in one of three directions: up, down, or sideways. Learning to identify these directions will help you navigate the market with greater confidence.

When the market is moving up, we are talking about an uptrend. In an uptrend, prices rise consistently, creating a series of higher highs and higher lows. This means that every time the price pulls back, it does not go down as much as it did in the previous pullback, and every time it moves up, it reaches a new high. This structure is key to identifying a bullish direction. In other words, the market shows a clear intention to go up, and buyers are the ones who are controlling the situation. In an uptrend, it is usually a good idea to look for buying opportunities, as the probability of the price continuing to rise is higher.

Conversely, when the market is moving downwards, it is a downtrend. In a downtrend, the price is steadily falling, creating a series of lower highs and lower lows. Here, the sellers are the ones in control, and the market shows a downward bias. Each time the price tries to rally, it fails to reach the level it was at before, and when it falls again, it sets a new low. This is a clear sign that the momentum is in favor of the sellers. In a downtrend, the best strategy is likely to be to look for selling opportunities or avoid buying until the market shows signs of reversal.

The third direction the market can take is sideways, meaning the price is moving in a range with no clear direction. This is what is known as a ranging or consolidating market. In this case, the price is not making higher highs or lower lows consistently. Instead, it is oscillating between a support level and a resistance level, as if it were stuck in a box.

During a consolidation, there is no clear winner between buyers and sellers. The market is waiting for something to happen to decide which direction to continue in. While this type of movement can be frustrating for some traders, it can also offer opportunities for those who know how to take advantage of breakouts when the market finally chooses a direction.

The key to reading market direction is to understand these three movements and be able to identify which one is happening at any given time. To do this, you don't need a bunch of indicators or complicated tools. All you need to do is look at the chart and focus on the price structure. By paying attention to the highs and lows that the market is forming, you can begin to recognize the pattern of an uptrend, a downtrend, or a sideways movement.

It is important to note that the market does not always move in a straight line. Even in an uptrend, there will be pullbacks, which are small downward movements within a larger upward movement. Likewise, in a downtrend, it is normal to see small spikes in price before it falls again. These pullbacks are a natural part of the market and do not mean that the trend has changed. Pullbacks can be opportunities to enter in the direction of the overall trend, as they often allow you to get a better price before the market continues in the same direction.

Another tool that can be helpful in reading market direction is identifying breakout points. Breakouts occur when the price breaks through a key support or resistance level, and they often signal a change in direction or a continuation of an existing trend. If the market has been consolidating for a while and then breaks above resistance, that could be a sign that buyers are taking over and the price could start to rise. Likewise, if the market breaks below support in a downtrend, that could signal that sellers are ready to push the price even further down.

A common mistake that many beginning traders make is trying to guess the top or bottom of the market – that is, trying to predict when an uptrend is going to reverse and start going down or when a downtrend is going to change and start going up. This type of trading is risky because trends can last much longer than you expect. Rather than trying to catch the perfect turnaround, it is more effective to follow the direction that is already developing. If the market is going up, it is wiser to look for buying opportunities. If the market is going down, it makes more sense to look for selling opportunities.

Something you should also keep in mind is that the market can change direction at any time, so it's important to always be on the lookout for signs that the market is losing steam in one direction and could be ready to turn around. Signs of exhaustion, such as a weakening at the highs or lows, or a candlestick pattern such as the "hammer" or "hanging man," can suggest that the trend is losing momentum and that you could see a change in direction soon. These signs aren't foolproof, but they can give you an idea that it's time to be on the alert.

Additionally, the direction of the market can vary depending on the time frame you are using. You might see an uptrend on a daily chart, but when looking at a 1-hour chart, you might see consolidation or even a downtrend. That is why it is important to keep the bigger picture in mind and not focus solely on a specific time frame. By looking at multiple time frames, you can get a clearer view of what is happening in the market and make more informed decisions.

In short, reading market direction doesn't have to be complicated. It's all about identifying whether the price is going up, down, or moving sideways. By looking at the structure of highs and lows, you can begin to recognize patterns that indicate the predominant direction. Whether you're trading in an uptrend, a downtrend, or a range-bound market, the important thing is to adapt to the situation and make decisions based on what the market is showing you. With practice, this skill will become a fundamental part of your trading strategy and will allow you to navigate the market with greater confidence.

Reversal and Continuation Patterns

Reversal and continuation patterns are essential tools in price action analysis. These patterns help us interpret what the market is doing and predict what might happen next. Knowing how to recognize them can make a big difference when making trading decisions, as they indicate whether a trend is about to reverse or is likely to continue. Although it may seem complicated at first, learning to identify these patterns is a skill that any trader can develop with practice and observation.

Let's start by talking about reversal patterns. As the name suggests, these patterns signal that the current market trend is losing steam and that a new trend in the opposite direction could begin instead. These patterns are particularly useful because they allow you to get ahead of trend changes, giving you the opportunity to enter the market at a good time before a new direction begins. Some of the most well-known reversal patterns are the double top, the double bottom, the head and shoulders, and its inverted version.

The double top pattern occurs in an uptrend when the price rises to a level, pulls back, and then rises back to the same level without being able to break above it. At that point, the price starts to fall, suggesting that buyers have lost strength and that sellers are taking over. Imagine this as a runner trying to jump over a high fence: he gets close, tries once, but fails. He tries again, but fails again, and finally gives up and pulls back. In the market, this means that the price is probably going to fall, and this double top pattern is usually a clear sign of a trend reversal from bullish to bearish.

In contrast, the double bottom pattern occurs in a downtrend. The price drops to a level, bounces back up, but then drops back down to the same level without being able to break it. Failing to break that support level, the price starts to rise again. This pattern is a sign that sellers are losing strength and that buyers could take over, leading to a potential bullish reversal. It's as if the price finds a solid "floor" at that level and can't go any lower, indicating that we're likely to see a rally in the near future.

Another very common reversal pattern is the head and shoulders, which appears at the end of an uptrend. This pattern forms when the price rises and reaches a high (left shoulder), then pulls back a bit, rises again and reaches a higher high (head), then falls again, and finally rises once more but fails to break above the first high (right shoulder). This pattern indicates that the bullish momentum is running out and that the trend could reverse to a bearish one. The head and shoulders is one of the most reliable reversal patterns, as it usually anticipates significant changes in the market.

The inverted head-and-shoulders is the opposite version and occurs in a downtrend. Here, the price makes a low (left shoulder), bounces, falls to a lower low (head), bounces again, and then falls once more but fails to make a new low (right shoulder). This pattern suggests that sellers are losing strength and that buyers might be ready to take over, indicating a possible bullish reversal. Like the head-and-shoulders, this inverted version is very useful in identifying changes in the trend.

Now let's talk about continuation patterns, which are equally important. While reversal patterns tell you that the current trend could change, continuation patterns suggest that the current trend is strong and likely to continue. These patterns are valuable because they allow you to find times when it is safe to join an already established trend, which is a key strategy in trading. Some of the most common continuation patterns include triangles, flags, and rectangles.

One of the most well-known continuation patterns is the triangle. There are three main types of triangles: symmetrical, ascending, and descending. The symmetrical triangle occurs when the price moves in a narrowing range, forming a sort of triangle on the chart. This means that both buyers and sellers are losing strength, but neither has gained full control. Eventually, the price will break out of this triangle, and it is likely to continue in the direction of the previous trend. This pattern is useful because it suggests that the market is in a temporary pause before continuing with its original move.

The ascending triangle occurs in an uptrend. In this pattern, the price forms a series of equal highs at the top and ascending lows at the bottom, indicating that buyers are pushing the price up, but sellers are trying to keep it within a range. Eventually, the price breaks the resistance at the top and the uptrend continues. This pattern is a clear signal that buyers are gaining strength and the price is likely to continue rising.

On the other hand, the descending triangle is the opposite version. It forms in a downtrend, with a series of equal lows at the bottom and descending highs at the top. Here, sellers are pushing the price down, while buyers try to keep the price within a range. However, sellers usually win this battle, and the price breaks the support at the bottom to continue its downtrend.

Another very useful continuation pattern is the flag. Flags are small corrections in price that occur within a strong trend. Imagine that the price has been rising rapidly and then pauses, moving sideways or slightly downwards before resuming its rise. This corrective move, which looks like a flag waving on a flagpole, is what is known as a flag. Flags indicate that the market is simply taking a breather before continuing in the same direction. By identifying a flag, you can take advantage of the opportunity to enter the trend just when the market is ready to continue.

Finally, we have the rectangle pattern, which is also a continuation pattern. The rectangle is formed when the price moves within a range defined by a horizontal support and resistance. As the price oscillates between these levels, it appears to be "stuck" in a channel. However, this pattern usually appears during a pause in a trend, and eventually the price breaks out of the rectangle in the direction of the previous trend. The rectangle pattern is a sign that the market is consolidating before continuing its previous move.

It's important to remember that no pattern is foolproof. While reversal and continuation patterns can give you a good idea of what might happen, it's always advisable to combine them with other tools and signals to confirm your analysis. Sometimes, the market can act unexpectedly and break a pattern, and that's something every trader should be prepared to handle. However, mastering the art of recognizing these patterns can give you a significant advantage in your market analysis.

In short, reversal and continuation patterns are powerful tools for any trader who wants to base their decisions on price action. Reversal patterns help you spot when a trend is losing steam and is likely to change direction, while continuation patterns tell you that the current trend is strong and likely to continue. By learning to identify these patterns, you will not only improve your ability to read the market, but you will also be able to make more informed decisions and take advantage of more profitable trading opportunities. With time and practice, these patterns will become a fundamental part of your trading strategy.

Volatility Reading and Trading Ranges

Reading volatility and trading ranges is a key part of price action analysis, as it helps you understand how the market is moving and how quickly those moves are happening. Volatility, in simple terms, refers to how much the price changes over a given period of time. When the market is volatile, it means that the price is going up and down quickly, while in a market with low volatility, price movements are slower and smaller. Understanding volatility is essential because it can directly influence your trading decisions. If the market is highly volatile, you might expect larger and faster moves, which can offer opportunities, but also carry higher risks. On the other hand, in a market with low volatility, the moves are often more predictable, although the opportunities may be less exciting.

One of the first things you need to understand about volatility is that it doesn't always stay the same. Sometimes, the market is in what we might call a quiet phase, where the price barely moves. Other times, it seems to be on a roller coaster, with sharp ups and downs. Volatility tends to be cyclical: periods of low volatility are often followed by periods of high volatility, and vice versa. This happens because the market goes through consolidation and expansion phases. During consolidation phases, the price moves within a narrow range, and volatility is low. In expansion phases, the price breaks out of that range and starts moving faster, which creates more volatility.

To measure volatility, many traders turn to tools like Bollinger Bands or the Average True Range (ATR) indicator. However, even without using indicators, you can get a good idea of volatility by simply looking at the size of the candles on the chart. When you see large, long-bodied candles, that usually indicates high volatility. Conversely, when candles are small and tightly spaced together, it's a sign that the market is calm and volatility is low. Learning to visually identify these changes in candle size will help you adjust your trading approach to current market conditions.

Volatility can be both an opportunity and a threat. If you're a trader looking for big moves in short periods of time, high volatility may be just what you need. During such times, the market can move quickly in your favor, allowing you to make profits more quickly. However, it's important to note that high volatility also means higher risk. Just as price can move in your favor quickly, it can also go against you just as quickly. That's why, during periods of high volatility, many traders choose to reduce their position sizes or adjust their stop loss levels to protect themselves from unexpected sharp moves.

On the other hand, when volatility is low, the market tends to move in a more predictable manner. During these periods, it is common to see the price stay within a well-defined range. A trading range is simply the area between a support level and a resistance level where the price oscillates. In a range-bound market, the price repeatedly moves up and down within these boundaries with no clear direction. This type of movement is often frustrating for those looking for big trends, but it can be a great opportunity for traders who prefer to trade within ranges, buying at support and selling at resistance.

Identifying a trading range is relatively straightforward. On a chart, you'll see that the price keeps bouncing between two clearly defined levels without breaking them. The support level is the point at which the price stops falling and starts to rise, while the resistance level is the point at which the price stops rising and starts to fall. During a range-bound market, the price tends to move between these two points over and over again, offering opportunities to enter and exit on each bounce. However, it's important to keep an eye out for potential breakouts of this range, as eventually the market will break out of its consolidation phase and start to move more aggressively in one direction.

An interesting aspect of trading ranges is that they can be either horizontal or sloping. Horizontal ranges are the easiest to identify, as support and resistance are aligned in a parallel fashion. However, you may also come across sloping ranges, where the price is gradually moving up or down within a channel. These sloping ranges are also trading opportunities, as the price is still moving within certain predictable boundaries, but with a slightly more defined direction than a horizontal range.

When trading in a market with well-defined ranges, the key is to be patient and wait for the price to reach support or resistance levels before taking a position. Many traders make the mistake of entering in the middle of the range, which leaves them vulnerable to sudden moves in either direction. Instead, the ideal strategy is to buy near support and sell near resistance, or vice versa if you're looking to short. This way, you maximize your chances of success, as you're taking advantage of key points where the price is most likely to bounce.

Another important aspect to consider when you are analyzing volatility and trading ranges is the market context. Volatility is not the same in all markets or at all times of the day. For example, currency pairs such as EUR/USD tend to be more volatile during the European and American session, while volatility decreases during the Asian session. The same goes for other assets, such as stocks or commodities. Understanding when the market is most volatile during the day will help you adjust your strategies and avoid surprises. Also, certain economic events, such as the release of important reports or decisions by central banks, can dramatically increase market volatility in a short period of time. That is why it is essential to keep abreast of the economic calendar and be aware of events that could affect the market you are trading.

When volatility suddenly increases, it is common to see breakouts of trading ranges. A breakout occurs when the price finally breaks out of the range it has been consolidating in and begins to move more aggressively in one direction. Breakouts are often accompanied by an increase in volatility as more traders join the move once it has been confirmed. This can be a great opportunity for those who prefer to trade stronger trends, but it is also a time when you should be cautious as false breakouts are common. A false breakout occurs when the price appears to be breaking out of a range, but then turns around and re-enters the range, trapping those who were quick to enter the market.

One of the ways experienced traders deal with volatility and ranges is by adjusting their strategy based on the context. During periods of low volatility, they may choose to trade within the range, while during periods of high volatility, they prefer to wait for breakouts and ride the trend. Additionally, it is common for them to adjust their position sizes and the risk they take based on market volatility. If volatility is high, they may reduce their position sizes to limit risk, while if volatility is low, they may increase their position sizes to maximize their profits in a more predictable market.

In short, reading volatility and trading ranges is an essential skill for any trader. Volatility tells you how quickly and aggressively the market is moving, which can directly influence your decision-making. A volatile market can offer great opportunities, but it also carries greater risks. On the other hand, trading ranges are well-defined areas where the price oscillates between support and resistance levels. Trading within these ranges can be a profitable strategy, as long as you are patient and wait for the price to reach the key levels. In any case, understanding the context and adjusting your approach based on volatility and ranges will help you navigate the market more effectively and make more informed trading decisions.

Interpreting Volume with Price Action

Volume is one of the most important tools you can use when analyzing price action. In simple terms, volume shows us how many assets, such as stocks, futures contracts, or units of a currency, are being bought and sold in a given period. It's like a magnifying glass that allows you to see the amount of activity behind market movements. It's often said that price is the "what" and volume is the "how." This means that while price tells you where the market is moving, volume gives you a clue as to how strong or weak that movement is. The higher the volume, the more significant the price direction is.

To begin to understand the relationship between volume and price action, you need to remember that not all price moves are created equal. A price increase on low volume does not have the same force as a price increase on high volume. High volume indicates that there are more participants in the market, which reinforces the legitimacy of the move. It's like watching a race: if there's only one runner on the track, it's probably not a very exciting competition. But if you see hundreds of runners, then you know it's a serious race. Likewise, when volume is high, you can be more confident that the price move has solid backing.

One of the basic principles in interpreting volume is that when price rises in conjunction with an increase in volume, it is a sign that the uptrend is strong and likely to continue. This is because many buyers are entering the market, which pushes the price up. But if price rises and volume does not match that move, it is a warning. Lack of volume suggests that there is not enough buying interest to sustain the rise, and this could mean that the uptrend is losing steam. In other words, a price rise with low volume is like building a house on sand: it looks stable on the outside, but it does not have a firm foundation.

The same is true in a downtrend. If the price is falling and the volume is increasing, it indicates that the downtrend is strong, as there are many sellers who are willing to get rid of their assets. However, if the price is falling but the volume is low, the downtrend may not be as strong as it seems, and there is a chance that the price will bounce back soon. This type of analysis can help you anticipate possible reversals in the market.

Another important aspect of volume is how it behaves at key support and resistance zones. Imagine that the price has been moving up and is right at a major resistance level. This is where volume becomes really useful. If the price breaks the resistance with a significant increase in volume, it is a sign that buyers are in control and we will likely see a continuation of the uptrend. Volume confirms that the breakout is real. But if the price breaks the resistance with low volume, the breakout may be a false breakout, meaning that the price could fall back below the resistance level.

Similarly, at a support level, if the price is falling and reaches that level with increasing volume, you might see a break of the support, which would indicate that sellers are in control. But if the price reaches the support and the volume decreases, it is a sign that sellers are losing strength and that the support could hold, which could lead to a reversal to the upside. In these cases, volume acts as a filter that allows you to differentiate between moves that are legitimate and those that are not.

In addition to breakouts, another interesting pattern you can analyze with volume is divergence. A divergence occurs when price and volume are not in sync. For example, imagine that price continues to rise, but volume is decreasing. This is a bearish divergence, and it usually indicates that the uptrend is losing steam and a reversal could soon occur. Conversely, if price is falling but volume is also decreasing, this could be a sign that sellers are losing momentum, which could lead to a bullish reversal. Divergences between price and volume can be powerful warning signals for impending changes in market direction.

Volume analysis not only helps you confirm price moves, but it also gives you an idea of when the market might be about to pause or reverse. A useful concept here is that of a "volume climax." A volume climax occurs when trading volume reaches extremely high levels, indicating exhaustion in the current trend. In a selling climax, for example, volume increases significantly while the price continues to fall. This suggests that selling pressure has peaked, and that the market is likely preparing to bounce. Similarly, a buying climax occurs when volume spikes during an uptrend, indicating that buyers might be exhausted and a correction could be near.

It is also important to understand that volume is not always the same at all times of the day or across all markets. For example, in the forex market, volume tends to be highest during the European and American sessions, when markets are most active. In contrast, during the Asian session, volume is often lower, which can lead to less significant price movements. Similarly, in the stock market, volume tends to be highest at the beginning and end of the session, with a decline during midday. By taking these patterns into account, you can adjust your trading expectations and strategies based on expected volume behavior.

It is important to remember that volume alone is not always enough to make trading decisions. While it can give you a good indication of the strength behind a move, it is always better to combine it with other tools and analysis. Some traders prefer to use volume in conjunction with technical indicators such as the moving average or RSI to confirm their analysis. In this way, volume becomes another piece of the puzzle that helps you build a more complete picture of the market.

Finally, you should keep in mind that volume can be interpreted in different ways depending on the type of asset you are trading. In the stock market, for example, volume is a clear indicator of the amount of shares being bought and sold. In the futures market, volume reflects the number of contracts changing hands. In the forex market, however, there is no centralized volume because the market is decentralized. Instead, traders often use volume indicators based on the number of ticks or price movements. While not a perfect representation of actual volume, this approach can still provide useful clues about activity in the market.

In short, volume interpretation is a crucial tool for any trader looking to make informed decisions based on price action. Volume helps you understand how strong a price move is, provides you with clues about potential reversals, and allows you to identify when a breakout is real or false. By learning to analyze volume in combination with price, you can gain an edge in the market as it gives you additional information that simple price movement alone cannot offer. While volume is not foolproof, it is one of the most powerful tools at your disposal, and with time and practice, it will become an integral part of your trading approach.

Price Action Based Risk Management

Risk management is undoubtedly one of the most important and least glamorous aspects of trading, but mastering it can make the difference between success and failure. When we talk about managing risk based on price action, we are referring to making strategic decisions to protect our capital based on the movements we see on the charts. In other words, we use the market's behavior, reflected in the price, to determine how much we are willing to risk on each trade and when is the right time to enter or exit a position.

The first step to managing risk is to understand that the goal in trading is not simply to make money, but to preserve your capital. It doesn't matter how accurate your predictions are if you risk too much on a single trade. Markets can be unpredictable, and even the most experienced traders have losing streaks. That's why it's essential to limit your risk on each trade. Many professional traders recommend not risking more than 1% or 2% of your account on a single trade. This means that if you have a $10,000 account, you shouldn't be willing to lose more than \$100 or \$200 on any one trade, no matter how confident you are about the outcome.

This is where price action comes into play. By analyzing charts, you can identify key points that will help you determine where to place your stop loss orders, which are a crucial tool for limiting losses. A stop loss is simply an order that automatically closes your position when the price reaches a certain level against you. For example, if you buy an asset at \$50 and decide that you don't want to lose more than \$5 on that trade, you could place your stop loss at \$45. This way, if the market moves against you, your position will automatically be closed before the losses become too great.

But how do you know where to place that stop loss? This is where price action analysis becomes valuable. Instead of just picking an arbitrary number, you can use support and resistance levels to place your stop loss more strategically. A support level is an area on the chart where the price has tended to stop when it falls, while a resistance level is where the price tends to stop when it rises. If you're buying an asset, you might place your stop loss just below a major support level. The logic behind this is that if the price falls below that level, the trend is likely to change, and you'd rather exit the trade before you suffer further losses.

On the other hand, if you are shorting, i.e. betting that the price is going to go down, you might place your stop loss just above a key resistance level. If the price breaks through that resistance, it is a sign that the market could be heading higher, and you will want to close your position before losses increase. Using these support and resistance levels based on price action gives you an advantage because you are not placing your orders randomly, but rather based on historical market behavior.

Another crucial aspect of risk management is adjusting your position size based on where you place your stop loss. This means that if you decide that your stop loss needs to be further away from the current price to give the market more room to move, you should reduce your position size to keep your risk under control.

For example, if you normally risk $100 on a trade, but this time you need a wider stop loss, then you could reduce the amount of assets you buy so that even if the price moves to your stop loss, you only lose that $100.

Similarly, if you can place a closer stop loss because you have identified a very clear support or resistance level, then you might be able to increase your position size because you are risking less in terms of points. This allows you to maximise your potential profits without increasing your overall risk. The key here is that you should always adjust your position size based on the distance between your entry price and your stop loss level, keeping the risk constant on each trade.

In addition to using stop losses, you can also use the concept of "risk-reward ratio" to better manage risk in your trades. The risk-reward ratio measures how much you are willing to risk compared to how much you expect to gain. A risk-reward ratio of 1:2 means that you are willing to risk $1 to gain $2. Ideally, you should always look for trades with a favorable risk-reward ratio, because even if you don't win all of your trades, your gains will outweigh your losses in the long run.

For example, if you enter a trade and you are risking $100, you should be looking for a potential profit of at least $200. This allows you to be profitable even if you are only right on 50% of your trades. By maintaining a favorable risk-reward ratio, you also avoid the temptation to hold onto a losing position in the hope that the market will eventually move in your favor. Instead, you close your losses early and allow your winning trades to run, which is one of the keys to trading success.

An often overlooked aspect of risk management is the importance of patience. Many traders are tempted to enter the market as soon as they see an opportunity, but it is crucial to wait for the price to reach the levels you have identified as important. If the market is not aligned with your criteria, it is better not to trade than to enter a trade that does not have a good chance of success. Learning to be patient and wait for the right setups based on price action will help you reduce risk and improve your long-term results.

Another vital component of risk management is not overtrading. Sometimes traders feel the need to be constantly in the market, which can lead to rash and risky decisions. However, in trading, less is often more. It is better to make a few high-quality trades with controlled risk than to constantly trade with mediocre results. Not only does this protect your capital, but it also helps you maintain a more focused and less emotional mindset. Overtrading can be mentally and emotionally draining, which can lead to costly mistakes.

Furthermore, it is important to recognize that the market will not always align with your analysis or strategy. Sometimes, you will have losing streaks, and that is completely normal. The most important thing is not to let a series of losses affect your confidence or lead you to make impulsive decisions to try to quickly recover what you lost. Risk management protects you precisely at these times. If each loss is well controlled, no losing streak should seriously affect your account. With price action as a guide, you can identify when it is prudent to reduce your position size or even stay out of the market for a while if conditions are not favorable.

One of the keys to good risk management is to always maintain an objective mindset. Traders who make decisions based on emotion often fall into dangerous traps, such as moving their stop losses further out to avoid a loss or holding onto losing positions in the hope that the market will eventually turn in their favor. These impulsive decisions often lead to bigger losses. Instead, if you follow a plan based on price action and manage your risk in a disciplined manner, you will be better prepared to face the ups and downs of the market without compromising your trading account.

In conclusion, price action-based risk management is critical to protecting your capital and increasing your chances of trading success. By using support and resistance levels to place your stop losses, adjusting your position sizes based on that risk, and maintaining a favorable risk-reward ratio, you can minimize losses and maximize profits over time. Patience, discipline, and objectivity are essential qualities for any trader who wants to survive and thrive in the markets. By managing risk appropriately, you ensure that the inevitable losses are small and controlled, allowing you to stay in the game long enough to take advantage of profitable opportunities when they arise.

Trading Psychology and Price Action

Trading psychology is one of the most critical and often underrated aspects of trading. While you can learn to read charts and master price action, if you don't understand how your emotions influence your decisions, it can be very difficult to be successful in the long run. The market is unpredictable, and that can cause traders to feel fear, anxiety, or greed. These emotions, if not managed properly, can lead you to make impulsive, risky, or poorly thought-out decisions. That's why it's so important to learn to control your emotions and develop a strong mindset that allows you to follow your price action-based strategy in a disciplined manner.

Fear is one of the most common emotions experienced by traders. Sometimes, fear sets in before you enter a trade, causing you to doubt your analysis. Even when everything seems to be aligned in your favor based on price action, you might feel afraid of losing money. This can lead you to not open trades that would otherwise be profitable. Fear can also manifest itself during a trade. Imagine you enter a position and the market starts to move against you. While it may be normal for the price to fluctuate a bit before heading in the direction you had anticipated, fear can cause you to close the trade too early, accepting a small loss, only to see the market eventually go in the direction you had anticipated.

Greed is another dangerous emotion that can affect your trading decisions. This emotion usually arises when a trade goes in your favor and you see the profits starting to pile up. Instead of closing the trade and locking in those profits, you may be tempted to keep it open longer in the hopes of making even more. Greed can lead you to ignore the warning signals given to you by price action, and as a result, you could end up losing much of what you had won or, worse, turning a winning trade into a losing one. That's why it's crucial to know when is the right time to take profits and not let greed cloud your judgment.

Another emotion that influences many traders is frustration. This usually occurs when you experience a losing streak. Trading can be very frustrating, especially when you think you've done everything right and the market just doesn't move the way you expected. At these times, it's easy to fall into the temptation of making impulsive decisions to "win back" what you lost. This type of emotional reaction can lead to overtrading, i.e. entering too many trades without a clear or strategic reason. The price action may not be giving any valid signals, but frustration pushes you to keep trading, which often results in more losses. It's essential to remember that every loss is part of the trading process, and learning to accept losses as natural will help you stay calm and stick to your plan.

The key to overcoming these emotions and staying focused on price action is to have a solid trading plan and stick to it. A trading plan is basically a set of rules that you follow before, during, and after each trade. These rules should include how you are going to identify opportunities based on price action, how much you are going to risk on each trade, and when you are going to exit a trade, whether with a profit or a loss. By having a clear plan and sticking to it, you reduce the influence of emotions as you make decisions based on a rational approach rather than emotional impulses.

An important part of this trading plan should include how you are going to manage risk. As we saw in the previous chapter, good risk management is essential to protect your capital, but it also has a direct impact on your psychology. If you know that you are only risking a small portion of your account on each trade, it will be easier to handle losses without them affecting you emotionally. On the other hand, if you risk too much on a single trade, each loss can feel devastating, which will increase your stress levels and lead you to make impulsive decisions on future trades.

It's also important to have realistic expectations. Many beginning traders come into the market with the idea that they're going to get rich quick. However, trading is a marathon, not a sprint. Price action can provide you with plenty of opportunities, but not all of them will result in winning trades. Having a 50% or 60% success rate can be enough to be profitable if you manage your risk well and allow your winning trades to cover the losses of the ones that don't work out. If you go into the market expecting to win on every trade, you'll quickly become frustrated and it'll be harder to stay calm when you're faced with a losing streak.

Another important aspect of trading psychology is patience. Price action is not always going to give you clear signals straight away, and sometimes you will need to wait before the market reaches the levels you have identified as key. It can be tempting to jump into the market too soon, especially when you feel like you are missing out on an opportunity, but this impatience can cost you dearly. Patience is essential in trading, as waiting for the right time to enter a trade can make the difference between a profitable trade and a losing one. Developing this patience requires discipline, but in the long run it is a skill that will protect you from making costly mistakes.

The right trading mindset also involves being flexible and willing to adapt. The market is constantly moving, and it's not always going to do what you expect. Sometimes, price action can signal that a trade that looked promising no longer is. In these cases, it's important to be humble enough to admit that you were wrong and exit the trade before losses mount up. Many traders hold on to a losing trade in the hope that the market will turn around, which can lead to big losses. Being flexible means being willing to adjust your strategy when the situation calls for it, without becoming emotionally attached to a position.

A useful technique to improve your trading psychology is to keep a trading journal. In this journal, you can record every trade you make, including why you made it, how you felt during the trade, and what you learned from it. This allows you to review your decisions objectively and spot patterns in your emotional behavior. For example, you might notice that you tend to close trades too early when you feel anxious or that you tend to increase your position size after a series of gains, which can be a sign of greed. By being aware of these emotional patterns, you can work to correct them and improve your decision making.

A common mistake traders, especially beginners, make is to focus solely on profits and losses, without paying enough attention to the quality of their decisions. The truth is that you can make an excellent trading decision and still lose money, because the market is unpredictable. Likewise, you could make a bad decision and end up making money simply because you got lucky. Instead of judging yourself on results alone, it's important to evaluate whether you followed your trading plan and made decisions based on price action, not emotions. If you focus on doing the right thing over and over again, positive results will come in the long run.

In addition to keeping your emotions in check while trading, it's also important to maintain a mental balance outside of the market. Trading can be emotionally draining, and if you focus too much on the ups and downs of the market, it can take a toll on your overall well-being. It's crucial to have a balanced life, where trading is just one part of your day. This can include exercising, spending time with family and friends, or pursuing hobbies you enjoy. A healthy body and mind will help you stay calm and clear when trading, which in turn will allow you to make better decisions based on price action.

Finally, remember that trading is a continuous learning journey. No matter how long you've been in the markets, there will always be something new to learn. Developing the right psychology for trading doesn't happen overnight. It takes time, experience, and self-reflection. The more you practice controlling your emotions and staying true to your price action-based strategy, the easier it will be for you to navigate the ups and downs of the market without your emotions dominating your decisions. Over time, you'll learn to view the market more objectively and make informed decisions that will allow you to grow as a trader and, most importantly, protect your capital while seeking profitable opportunities.

Operating in Times of News and Events

Trading in times of news and events can be one of the most exciting, but also one of the most challenging experiences for any trader. Financial markets are highly sensitive to news, whether it is a major economic report, a monetary policy decision, or even an unexpected comment from a world leader. These events can cause significant price movements, which creates both opportunities and risks for traders who trade based on price action. Understanding how to react to these events and how to use price action to guide your decisions can make the difference between success and loss in times of high volatility.

When major news is announced, markets often react quickly and sometimes unpredictably. Imagine you're looking at a candlestick chart just before a key interest rate announcement. You might notice that the market is quiet, with the candles showing little movement and a narrow price range. But once the news is out, the market can explode in one direction or another, creating large candles with long wicks and fast movements. These movements can be tempting for a trader, as the possibility of capturing a large profit in a short period is very attractive. However, this type of price action can be deceptive, as the volatility that follows the news can cause the market to change direction quickly, catching traders off guard.

One of the biggest challenges of trading during news events is that market movements are often driven by emotional reaction of participants, rather than rational analysis. Many traders, both novice and experienced, may act impulsively when a news story is released, entering trades out of fear of missing out on a major move. However, trading based solely on emotion or general market panic can be dangerous. Instead of making hasty decisions, it is better to wait for price action to give you clear signals of how the market is adjusting to the new information. A good strategy is to watch for early reactions and then wait for the market to stabilize before entering a trade.

One approach that many traders use is to trade "on the sidelines" of news events. This means being aware of when major news is going to be announced, but avoiding opening new trades just before or immediately after the announcement. This approach is particularly useful if you are inexperienced in trading in high volatility conditions, as it reduces the risk of being caught in unexpected moves. Instead of trying to guess how the market will react, you can wait for volatility to subside as price action gives you clearer signals. Patience is key in these types of situations, as although it can be tempting to try to take advantage of quick moves, waiting for the dust to settle will allow you to make more rational, less impulsive decisions.

For traders who prefer to take a more active approach during news events, the key is to be prepared and know what kind of reaction you might expect from the market. Each type of news affects the markets differently. For example, a jobs report could have a big impact on the currency market, while an interest rate decision could cause significant moves in the bond and stock markets. By knowing what to expect and having a plan of action based on price action, you can reduce uncertainty and increase your chances of success. It is important to study how the markets have reacted in the past to similar events, as this can give you insight into how you might react in the future.

Another thing to keep in mind is that spreads tend to increase during times of high volatility. This means that the cost of entering and exiting a trade can be much higher than usual, which can impact your profitability. Before trading during a news event, it is important to check the spread and make sure that it is not so wide that it prevents you from profiting from a favorable price movement. Also, because of how quickly prices move during these events, your stop-loss orders may not be executed at the exact price you expected, which could result in larger losses than anticipated. Taking these factors into account is essential to effectively managing risk when trading during news events.

Using pending orders can also be a useful strategy during news events. Pending orders allow you to place a trade before an event occurs, and these are triggered only if the market reaches a specific price. This can be useful if you anticipate the market will move in a particular direction, but you don't want to be in front of the screen at the exact moment of the announcement. For example, if you know that a key support or resistance level is near the current price, you could place a pending order at that level, trusting that price action will respect that zone even during the volatility caused by the news. However, this type of strategy is not without risk, as the market could quickly move against your trade before you can react.

It's also important to be aware of the concept of market "overreaction." Often, markets tend to overreact to news, creating extreme moves that don't always reflect the true impact of the information. For example, a negative economic report might cause a dramatic drop in stock prices, but soon after, the market might quickly recover as traders reconsider the significance of the news. That's why it's essential to keep the broader market context in mind and not get carried away by the first moves. Price action can help you identify when the market has overreacted and when it's the right time to enter a trade.

Another useful strategy during news events is to trade based on market expectations. Often, prices will have already priced in the potential news before it is officially announced. This means that if the news is exactly what the market expected, the impact on prices may be less than you might think. Conversely, if the news is unexpected or contrary to what most traders anticipated, the market movement may be much more violent. For example, if the market expects a company to announce good financial results and that is already reflected in the share price, the price action might show little reaction if the results are as good as expected. However, if the results are worse than expected, the price action could quickly move lower.

One of the biggest advantages of trading price action in times of news is that it allows you to follow what the market is doing in real time, without the need to rely on technical indicators that might lag. Price action is pure and direct, allowing you to see how market participants are reacting at that very moment. This gives you an advantage over those traders who rely too much on indicators that do not always reflect the reality of the market in times of high volatility. By focusing on price action, you can make quick decisions based on what is actually happening in the market, not what an indicator tells you should be happening.

In short, trading in times of news and events is an exciting but risky activity. The volatility that follows these events can create great opportunities, but it can also lead to losses if not managed properly. The key is to be prepared, have a clear trading plan based on price action, and be disciplined to not let emotions or panic influence your decisions. Whether you prefer to avoid these moments or take advantage of them, price action will provide you with the tools necessary to interpret market behavior and make informed decisions.

How to Use Timeframes in Price Action

Using time frames in price action is one of the most important tools for any trader, as it allows you to analyze the market from different perspectives and make more informed decisions. A time frame, also known as a "time frame," simply refers to the amount of time that each candle or bar on a chart represents. For example, on a 5-minute chart, each candle shows price movement over a five-minute period. If you switch to a 1-hour chart, each candle represents a full hour of price action. Depending on which time frame you choose, the chart can give you a different view of the market. Learning to use multiple time frames is key to getting a clearer picture of what's going on and making more accurate trading decisions.

The first thing you need to understand is that there is no "right" or "wrong" time frame for trading. Every trader has their own style and preferences. Some traders prefer shorter time frames, such as 1-minute or 5-minute charts, where price action moves quickly, and entry and exit opportunities are frequent. These traders are often known as "scalpers," as they look to make small but quick profits. Others prefer longer time frames, such as 1-hour, 4-hour, or even daily charts, where trends are clearer and there is more time to analyze the market before making a decision. This style is most common among "swing" traders, who look to capture larger moves and hold their positions open for days or weeks.

One of the benefits of using multiple time frames is that it allows you to get a more complete view of the market. For example, if you're trading on a 15-minute chart, you might identify a short-term trend, but if you switch to a 4-hour chart, you might discover that trend is just a small part of a larger move in the opposite direction. By using longer time frames alongside shorter ones, you can avoid falling into traps and gain a better understanding of major trends and key levels. A commonly used approach is to start with a longer time frame to identify the overall trend, and then switch to a shorter time frame to find entry opportunities based on price action.

One of the most effective strategies when using time frames is "top-down" analysis. This technique involves starting by looking at a larger time frame, such as a daily or 4-hour chart, to identify the main market direction. On this time frame, you can look for price action patterns, such as candlestick formations, support and resistance zones, or the direction of the trend. Once you have identified the overall trend, you can move down to a shorter time frame, such as the 1-hour or 15-minute chart, to look for entry opportunities. By doing this, you ensure that your trades are aligned with the main trend, which increases the likelihood of success.

Imagine, for example, that you are looking at a daily chart and you see that the market has been in an uptrend for several weeks, with the price rising consistently. This tells you that the overall market momentum is positive. You then switch to a 1-hour chart and notice that the price has been pulling back, but appears to be forming a key support zone. This pullback could be an opportunity to enter a long trade, knowing that the main trend is up and that the price is likely to rise again. This type of combined timeframe analysis helps you find more accurate entry points and minimize the risk of trading against the trend.

When trading price action, it is also helpful to pay attention to how key support and resistance levels on larger time frames affect price action on smaller time frames. The support and resistance levels you identify on a 4-hour or daily chart are often stronger and more relevant than those you might find on a 5-minute chart. This is because more traders, including institutional traders, are looking at those levels on the longer time frames. If price approaches a resistance level on a daily chart, you are likely to see a reaction on the 15-minute chart, which could create an opportunity to enter a short trade at an opportune time.

On the other hand, it is also important to understand that each time frame has its own characteristics and can show you different facets of price action. On short time frames, such as the 1-minute or 5-minute time frame, price movements can be very fast and volatile. This means that the signals you see on these charts might be more likely to generate "noise"

– erratic movements that do not represent a true trend. Therefore, trading on short time frames requires close attention and the ability to make quick decisions. If you are a beginner, it may be better to start with longer time frames, where trends are clearer and you have more time to analyze before acting.

Additionally, using timeframes allows you to tailor your trading style to your daily routine and availability. If you don't have much time to spend in front of a screen, long timeframes such as 4-hour or daily charts may be more suitable as they don't require constant monitoring. You can analyze the market at the beginning of the day, identify key support and resistance levels, and place your trades without having to worry about small movements that occur during the day. On the other hand, if you have more time to dedicate to trading and enjoy the thrill of fast movements, short timeframes might be more suitable for you.

It is also important to mention that while using multiple time frames can be very useful, you should be careful not to fall into overanalysis.

Sometimes, constantly switching from one time frame to another can confuse you and make you second-guess your decisions. It is best to choose a couple of time frames that you are comfortable with and that suit your trading style. For example, if you prefer short-term trading, you can use a 4-hour chart to identify the main trend and a 15-minute chart to find your entries. If you prefer longer-term trading, you can use a daily chart to analyze the overall trend and a 1-hour chart for your trades.

Finally, a key aspect to keep in mind when using time frames is consistency. Regardless of the time frame you choose, it is important that you maintain the same logic and approach in your price action analysis. This means that if you identify a candlestick pattern on a 4-hour chart, such as a bullish hammer in a support zone, that same pattern should have the same meaning on a 15-minute chart. You should not change your interpretation just because the time frame is different. Price action remains valid and useful on any time frame, as long as you interpret it consistently and follow your trading rules.

In summary, using timeframes in price action is a powerful tool that allows you to view the market from different angles and make more informed decisions. By combining long and short timeframes, you can identify the main trend and find precise entry opportunities, increasing your chances of success. Whether you prefer fast or slow trading, timeframes allow you to adapt your strategy to your needs and lifestyle. The important thing is to maintain consistency in your analysis and avoid information overload that can lead to indecision. With practice and experience, you will learn to use timeframes effectively and make more confident trading decisions based on price action.

Intraday Trading with Price Action

Day trading, or "day trading," is a strategy in which traders buy and sell assets within a single trading day, with the goal of taking advantage of short-term price movements. Rather than holding positions for days, weeks, or months, day traders close all their trades before the end of the market session. This style of trading is very popular due to its dynamism and the opportunities it offers to generate quick profits. Price action, which is based on reading and analyzing pure market movements through charts, is a fundamental tool for day trading, as it allows traders to make quick and accurate decisions without the need to rely on complex or lagging indicators.

When day trading with price action, the focus is on analyzing short-term charts, such as 1-minute, 5-minute, or 15-minute charts, to identify patterns and signals that indicate possible market movements. Unlike long-term traders who study broad trends and make decisions based on market behavior on larger time frames, day traders focus on capturing small, fast movements. This means that they need to be extremely agile in their analysis and execution, as any delay can cause them to miss an opportunity or suffer a loss.

One of the most important aspects of day trading with price action is learning to identify key support and resistance levels on short time frames. These levels are areas where price tends to stop, bounce or change direction, and they often represent areas of interest for other traders. For example, on a 5-minute chart, you might notice that price has repeatedly touched a support level and failed to break it. This could indicate an opportunity to buy, as price action suggests that the market is unwilling to let price fall below that level. Likewise, if price has repeatedly hit a resistance level and failed to break it, you might consider selling, waiting for price to pull back from that point.

A key concept in day trading is "momentum," which refers to the speed and strength with which price is moving. Price action is great for measuring momentum, as it allows you to see in real time how the market is moving. If the candles on a 1-minute chart are elongated and have little retracement, this indicates strong momentum in that direction. Day traders can take advantage of these quick moves by entering a momentum trade, hoping to capture a portion of the move before it runs out. However, it is crucial to remember that momentum can change quickly, so it is important to always be alert and ready to adjust your strategy if the market changes direction.

Risk management is another essential component of intraday trading, and it's something that can't be taken lightly, especially when using price action. Since intraday movements can be fast and volatile, it's easy to lose more than you planned if you don't have a clear strategy for managing risk. One of the most effective ways to do this is by using stop-loss orders, which are pre-set orders to exit a trade if the price reaches a certain level against you. When trading with price action, a well-placed stop-loss can be just below a support level or above a resistance level, depending on whether you're buying or selling. This protects you in case the market doesn't move as you expected and helps you limit your losses.

A significant advantage of day trading with price action is that you don't need to rely on many technical indicators that are often slow or confusing. Indicators like the RSI, moving averages, or MACD can be helpful for some traders, but they also have a lag, meaning they might not show you the change in the market until it's too late. Instead, by trading only with price action, you are directly seeing how the market is behaving at that moment. You are analyzing the movements of the candles, the formations, the wicks, and the bodies of the candles, which gives you instant information about the supply and demand in the market. This allows you to react faster and more accurately.

In addition to support and resistance levels, another important concept in price action day trading is candlestick patterns. Candlestick patterns are repeating formations on charts that indicate possible changes in price direction. Some common patterns that day traders look for include the hammer, bullish or bearish engulfing, and shooting stars, among others. These patterns, when identified correctly, can provide clear signals of when to enter or exit a trade. For example, if you see a bullish engulfing pattern on a 5-minute chart right at a support level, this could be a sign that price is about to rise, and you could take advantage of that opportunity to buy.

Scalping is a very popular technique among day traders who use price action. This technique involves making multiple trades in a single day, seeking to make small profits from each trade. Scalping is based on the idea that it is easier to capture small market movements than large trends. Scalpers use very short time frame charts, such as 1 minute or 5 minute charts, to identify rapid changes in price action. Although the profits from each trade may be small, the goal is to accumulate several profitable trades throughout the day. It is a style of trading that requires focus, speed, and a strong ability to make quick decisions.

While day trading can be exciting, it also has its downsides. One of the main challenges is the stress it can bring. Because market movements are fast and decisions must be made in a matter of seconds, day traders often feel a great deal of pressure. This stress can lead to mistakes, such as entering a trade without properly analyzing the price action or exiting too early for fear of missing out on a small profit. The key to success in day trading is to stay calm, stick to your trading plan, and not let emotions control your decisions. Self-control is just as important as technique in this style of trading.

Another disadvantage is that day trading requires time and dedication. Unlike traders who trade on longer time frames and may check the market once or twice a day, day traders must be in front of a screen for the majority of the market session, constantly looking for opportunities and reacting to price movements. This can be exhausting and is not always compatible with other personal or work commitments. While day trading can be very profitable, it is also important to consider whether you have the time and energy to pursue this style of trading on a consistent basis.

Despite the challenges, day trading remains an attractive option for many traders, especially those who enjoy the adrenaline rush of fast market movements and the possibility of daily profits. Price action is the perfect tool for this style of trading, as it provides you with the most direct and accurate information about what is happening in the market in real time. With practice and discipline, you can learn to identify patterns and signals on short time frames, make quick decisions, and manage your risk effectively, allowing you to be successful in day trading.

In summary, day trading with price action is an exciting strategy that requires a precise and agile approach. By learning how to read charts, identify key support and resistance levels, and manage momentum, you can take advantage of rapid market movements to make profits. However, it is also important to properly manage risk and not let emotions get the better of you. The key to success in this type of trading is constant practice, patience, and the ability to make quick decisions based on price action.

Price Action in High Liquidity Markets

Price action in highly liquid markets is a fascinating and crucial aspect for traders, especially those looking to take advantage of precise and fast market movements. When we talk about high liquidity, we are referring to markets where there is a high trading volume, which means that it is easier to buy or sell an asset without causing a large impact on its price. Highly liquid markets, such as major Forex currency pairs (e.g. EUR/USD), stocks of large companies like Apple or Google, or futures on major indices like the S&P 500, tend to be very attractive to traders as they offer greater stability and lower transaction costs.

Trading in highly liquid markets has several advantages that can be leveraged through price action. First, high liquidity reduces "slippages," which are price movements that occur when the market moves unexpectedly when an order is executed. In less liquid markets, such as the stocks of smaller companies or less popular cryptocurrencies, this type of slippage can be frequent and detrimental to traders. However, in highly liquid markets, the price moves in a smoother and more controlled manner, making price action much more reliable. As a trader, this allows you to read charts more accurately, as sharp or erratic movements are less common.

One of the key elements of trading in highly liquid markets is that price action signals are often cleaner and more reliable. Support and resistance levels, for example, are more respected because there are more market participants keeping an eye on those same levels. Imagine a highly liquid currency pair like EUR/USD. If the price is touching a major support level, chances are a lot of institutional and retail traders are watching that same level. Because of the number of orders placed around those key points, the market is more likely to react with predictable moves. This gives you greater confidence when making decisions based on price action.

High liquidity also allows candlestick patterns, such as reversal and continuation patterns, to be more meaningful. In low liquidity markets, it is common to see candlesticks with long wicks and erratic movements due to a lack of orders in certain areas of the chart. This can make it more difficult to accurately interpret price action. In contrast, in a liquid market, candlesticks are often more consistent, making it easier to identify patterns such as the hammer, doji, or bearish or bullish engulfing. By observing these patterns in liquid markets, you can have more confidence that they are real signals and not anomalies caused by a lack of volume.

Additionally, high liquidity tends to reduce extreme volatility, which can be beneficial if you prefer more controlled trading. While some traders seek out volatile markets to capture large price moves in a short period of time, many others prefer the stability that liquid markets offer. This doesn't mean that liquid markets aren't volatile at certain times, especially during important events such as economic data releases or central bank decisions. However, under normal conditions, liquid markets offer more stable price action, allowing traders to focus on taking advantage of more predictable moves. This stability also makes risk management easier, as you're less likely to be faced with sudden, extreme moves that put your account at risk.

One of the downsides, or at least challenges, of trading in highly liquid markets is that opportunities to make large profits in short time frames can be more limited compared to less liquid and more volatile markets. However, price action is still a powerful tool in these markets. The key is to be patient and take advantage of the smaller but safer moves that tend to occur. Instead of looking for big price "explosions," you can focus on identifying short-term trends, consolidations, and breakouts that occur more consistently.

Another important aspect of price action in highly liquid markets is how quickly you can enter and exit trades. Since there are always a large number of buyers and sellers, orders are executed more accurately and quickly. This is especially useful for day traders or those looking to take advantage of fast movements. If the market is moving in your direction, you can enter and exit a trade without worrying about a lack of counterparties. In low-liquidity markets, it is sometimes difficult to find a buyer or seller at the price you want, which can lead to you having to accept a less favorable price. In liquid markets, this problem almost does not exist, allowing you to make decisions based on price action more quickly.

Risk management is another aspect that is facilitated in highly liquid markets. As mentioned before, support and resistance levels are usually more robust, allowing for more precise stop-loss orders to be placed. If the market is respecting an important support level, you can place your stop-loss just below that level, confident that the market is less likely to break through that point due to the large number of orders in that area. Likewise, when trading in liquid markets, it is easier to adjust your position size according to your risk management plan, as there is always enough volume for you to buy or sell the exact amount of assets you want without significantly altering the price.

Despite the advantages of high liquidity, it is also important to note that these markets tend to attract more experienced traders, including large investment funds and institutional traders. This means that you will be competing with participants who have access to advanced technologies, real-time analysis, and large amounts of capital. However, this should not discourage you. Price action remains one of the most democratic tools in the trading world, as it is based on patterns and movements that any trader can learn to identify, regardless of the size of their account or the resources they have at their disposal. The key is to be disciplined, follow your trading plan, and learn to read price action accurately.

An interesting aspect of liquid markets is that, although they are more stable, they can also react dramatically to macroeconomic events or major news. When this happens, market behavior can change rapidly, and it is at these times that price action becomes an invaluable tool. Large price movements in response to news can offer excellent opportunities to enter and exit the market if you know how to read price action. For example, an unexpected announcement from the Federal Reserve can cause the dollar to move sharply, and by watching how the candles on the chart react, you can identify opportunities to take advantage of that movement.

In summary, trading in highly liquid markets using price action has several advantages, such as greater accuracy in chart interpretation, reliability of key levels, and ease of entering and exiting trades quickly. Although you may not see large price movements all the time, liquid markets offer greater stability, allowing you to manage risk more effectively and take advantage of more predictable opportunities. As a trader, it is critical to learn how to read price action in these markets and develop a strategy that suits their unique characteristics. With proper practice and good risk management, you can be successful trading in highly liquid markets using price action as your primary analysis tool.

Creating Your Price Action Trading Plan

Creating a trading plan based on price action is one of the most important steps you can take as a trader. This plan will be your roadmap, the guide that will help you maintain discipline and make consistent decisions instead of reacting emotionally to market movements. While this may seem like a daunting task, it doesn't have to be. What you need is a clear and simple approach that will help you understand how price action can guide your daily trading.

The first step in creating your trading plan is to set your goals. Ask yourself: What do I want to achieve with my trading? It can be as simple as generating additional income or as ambitious as making a living solely from trading. No matter what your goal is, the important thing is that it is clear, realistic and measurable. Having a well-defined goal will give you clear motivation and help you evaluate your progress over time. It will also help you stay focused, even in times when the market is not moving the way you expect.

Once you've defined your goals, it's time to develop a strategy based on price action. This is where you start to lay out the rules you'll follow when looking at charts and making buy or sell decisions. The first thing you need to decide is what time frames you're going to use. Price action can be applied on any time frame, from one-minute charts to daily or weekly charts. However, your choice of time frame will depend on your trading style. If you're an intraday trader, you'll probably focus on 5- to 15-minute charts. If you prefer a more relaxed approach, you might use daily or even weekly charts. Whatever you choose, make sure your time frame is aligned with your lifestyle and trading goals.

Another key aspect of your price action trading plan is identifying the patterns that will guide your decisions. What patterns are you looking for? These could be reversal patterns like the hammer or shooting star, or continuation patterns like flags or triangles. It's important to define precisely what signals you're going to use and how you're going to interpret them. There's no point in looking for every possible pattern on a chart, as this will only lead to confusion and doubt. Instead, pick a couple of patterns that you understand well and focus on learning how to recognize them effectively. Remember that less is more when it comes to trading.

Part of your strategy should also include identifying key zones. These are areas on the chart where the price has previously shown a significant reaction, such as support or resistance levels. Correctly identifying these zones will give you a considerable advantage, as these are points where the market tends to make important decisions. In your trading plan, you should detail how you will identify these levels and how you will act when the price reaches them. For example, you may decide that if the price hits a support level, you will look for a reversal signal before entering a trade. Or, if the price breaks a resistance zone, you will look for confirmation to enter a buy trade. Defining these rules will help you eliminate uncertainty when you are faced with these situations in real time.

An essential component of any trading plan is risk management. No matter how accurate you are at reading price action, there will always be times when the market doesn't move in your favor. That's why it's vital that you define in advance how much you're willing to risk on each trade. A commonly accepted rule is to not risk more than 1% or 2% of your total capital on a single trade. This ensures that a series of losing trades doesn't destroy your account. In your plan, you should detail not only how much you're going to risk, but also how you're going to place your stops. Stops are a crucial aspect of risk management, as they protect you from larger losses. Ideally, you should place your stops in logical places on the chart, such as below a support level or above a resistance level, depending on whether you're buying or selling.

The next step in creating your price action trading plan is to define how you are going to manage your trades once they are underway. This includes things like when to take profits and how to adjust your stops as the price moves in your favor. Many traders make the mistake of not having a clear plan for exiting their trades, which often results in them closing their positions too early or too late. It is advisable to have a predefined profit target, but also to be flexible depending on how the market develops. For example, if the price continues to move in your favor, you could adjust your stop to lock in your profits rather than exiting the trade straight away. Likewise, if you see that the price action is showing signs that the market is turning around, you can close your position before reaching your initial target to protect your profits.

Psychology is another factor you need to consider when creating your trading plan. Trading can be emotionally draining, especially when the market doesn't move the way you expect. In your plan, you should include a section that helps you maintain discipline and avoid impulsive decisions. This can include rules like not trading if you've had several consecutive losses or taking a break if you feel overwhelmed. The key is to be aware of your emotions and have a plan to manage them. This way, you'll be able to stay calm and stick to your strategy, even in times of high pressure.

Finally, don't forget to include a section in your plan dedicated to continuous review and improvement. Trading is a constant learning process, and what works today may not work tomorrow. That's why it's critical that you set aside time to review your trades on a regular basis. This will allow you to identify patterns in your behavior, improve your weak points, and adjust your strategy as needed. Price action is a dynamic tool, and your trading plan should be flexible enough to adapt to changing market conditions.

In short, creating a price action trading plan involves setting clear goals, defining a strategy based on key patterns and zones, managing risk effectively, and maintaining a disciplined mindset. By having a solid plan, you will be better prepared to navigate the ups and downs of the market and make informed decisions. With time and experience, this plan will become your best ally, helping you trade with confidence and consistency in any situation you face in the market.

9 798822 773825 7